Helping Children See Jesus

ISBN: 978-1-64104-123-2

Filling A Little Space

Author: Chrystal Stauffer
Illustrators/Computer Graphic Artists: Olivia and Bethany Moy

Neither Death Nor Life
The Love of Jim and Elisabeth Elliot

Author: Chrystal Stauffer
Illustrator/Computer Graphic Artist: Ben Schipper

Our Father's House
A Story of John Paton

Author: Hannah Landis
Illustrator/Computer Graphic Artist: Zachary Franzen

© 2020 Bible Visuals International
PO Box 153, Akron, PA 17501-0153
Phone: (717) 859-1131
www.biblevisuals.org

All rights reserved. No part of this publication may be reproduced, stored in a retrieval system or transmitted in any form by any means, electronic, mechanical, photocopy, recording or otherwise, without the prior permission of the publisher, except as provided by USA copyright law.

RELATED ITEMS

To access related items (such as activities, memory verse posters and translated texts) please visit our web store at shop.biblevisuals.org and enter 5720, 5740 or 5750 in the search box on the page.

FREE TEXT DOWNLOAD

To access a FREE printable copy of the teaching text (PDF format) in English or other available languages, enter S5720DL , S5740DL or S5750DL in the search box. Add the item to your cart, and use coupon code XTACSV17 at checkout. Once your order is processed you will receive an email with a link to the free download.

STUDENT ACTIVITES

These are included with the FREE printable copy of the English teaching text for this story. See the directions under Free Text Download (above) to access them.

TABLE OF CONTENTS

Filling a Little Space 1-15

Neither Death Nor Life 16-36

Our Father's House 37-51

Filling a Little Space

The Susanna Wesley Story

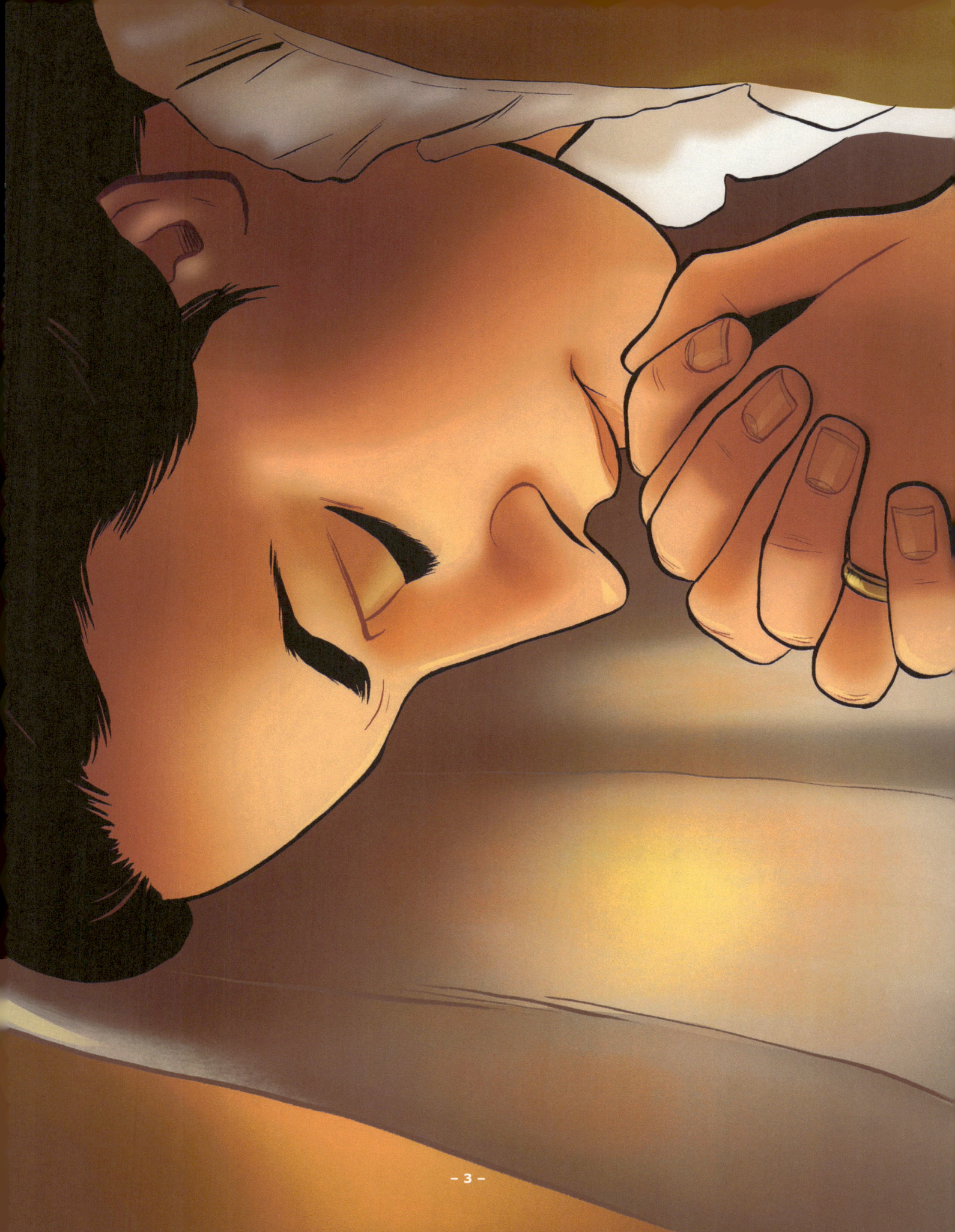

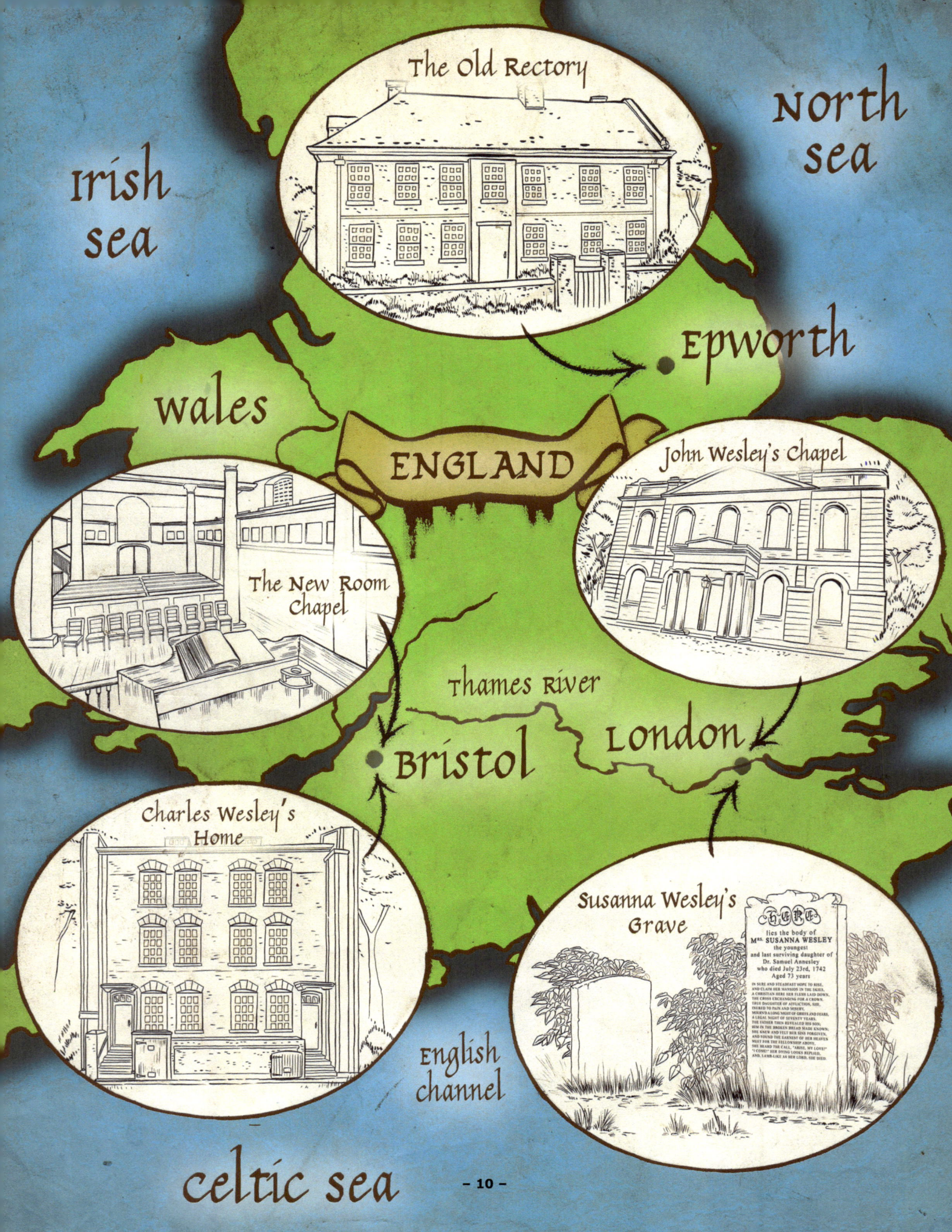

> **NOTE TO THE TEACHER**
> This story may be told in one, two or three sessions.
> The circle (●) indicates where to divide the narrative when teaching two sessions.
> The triangle (▶) indicates the breaks for three sessions.

Introduction

Susanna rubbed her swollen belly and wondered how much longer it would be before this little one decided to join them. She was seven months pregnant. Glancing around the small kitchen, she noticed that the fire burning in the brick fireplace needed stirred, the chairs needed straightened and her plant in the corner needed watered. *Those can wait*, she told herself as she thought about how little food they had on hand at the moment and that there would still be hungry little bellies to fill at dinner. She was just thankful they had a roof over their heads. They had been in debt for a long time, and it seemed that no matter what her husband Samuel did, they couldn't get ahead.

In 1697, they had moved to Epworth, Lincolnshire (show map) hoping to get a fresh start, but after more than ten years there they were still in debt. There was always another trip Samuel needed to take as the minister, another crop that had failed and yet another mouth to feed. Susanna didn't mind being poor, but she did hate it when people criticized her husband for not providing well for the family.

Yes, their house was small, their food scarce and their possessions few, but she was content. Her happiness came from knowing God and being known by Him. She prayed that her children would know this same happiness.

This baby she was carrying was number 19 for her and Samuel! Despite the fact she was weary and felt as if she'd been sick and pregnant for most of their married life, she wasn't going to take this little one for granted. Though illness, disease and tragedy common in those days, nine of her 19 children were already buried, most of them as infants, and Susanna knew that each day with her remaining children was a gift. She breathed a quick prayer. "Thank you, Lord. I know that 'tis no small honor to be entrusted with the care of so many souls."

* * * * *

Show Illustration #1

The kitchen door was suddenly flung open by Susanna's daughter Hetty. The girl paused in the doorway breathless. Susanna was about to scold her for disturbing the peace when she noticed that the girl's eyes were filled with tears. "Why, Hetty, whatever is the matter?" she questioned. "It's Father," Hetty wailed and her body shook with sobs. "Someone just came to say that they've taken him again!" "Who's taken him?" Susanna inquired calmly as she moved to her daughter's side. Hetty flung herself into the arms of her mother. "They've arrested him and said they are taking him to jail again because of his debt," Hetty finally managed to get out.

Susanna took a deep breath and quietly stroked her daughter's hair to calm her. It also gave her time to gather her own thoughts. This wasn't the first time Samuel had been arrested and taken to debtors' prison. Unless someone sent money to pay off the debt, he'd have to stay in the prison until he could work it off there. From around the corner of the hallway, she could see three or four more curious little faces sticking their heads out, watching the scene before them unfold. "Mother, are we really so poor? Can they just take Father away like that?" Hetty asked, lifting her head and sniffing. "Yes, Hetty, we are. And yes, they can." Susanna answered honestly. This brought more tears. "Oh why does this have to happen to us? What are we ever going to do? And Mother, what have we done to deserve this? Why does God allow such things to happen?" Hetty couldn't stop the questions from flowing. Susanna gently held Hetty at arm's length so she could look her in the face. "Listen, Hetty. As long as we have God, it doesn't really matter what's going on or where we are. God is enough. You must trust in His love and goodness. Now, dry your tears. We shall have no more of those. There is nothing we can do for the time being but wait to hear from your father."

Show Illustration #2

Suddenly feeling the strong need to pray, Susanna sent Hetty on her way before throwing her apron over her head and sinking onto a stool. Her children knew that they were not to disturb her whenever the apron was over her head, so she could be guaranteed some quiet for the time being.

Despite what she had said to Hetty, she could feel the discouragement and fear in her own heart. Many years on her knees had brought her to the realization that prayer was her greatest weapon during such battles. As a child, she'd made a commitment that for every hour she spent in entertainment, she would spend one hour with God in prayer and in the Word. Now, as an adult, she found this was impossible. Instead, she'd decided to spend two hours a day in prayer. In her mind, this was time well spent. So often she found herself needing wisdom or peace. *Oh God*, her heart moaned. *I know that You are here. Help me to endure this well. You know how much harder it is for me to feed the family when this happens. Help my children's faith in You to be strengthened through this trial as we see You provide once more. Lord, I am content to fill a little space if You are glorified.*

An hour later, Susanna rose from the stool feeling much refreshed. God was able. He would carry them through. And carry them He did. After a few weeks in prison, Samuel was released due to various people's sending money on his behalf.

However, their troubles were far from over.

One night after everyone had long been asleep, Susanna's eyes flew open, and she bolted upright in the bed. What had awakened her? She could hear Hetty's voice calling out loudly and urgently. She took a brief moment to gather her bearings, then she smelled it. Smoke! Something was burning! She stumbled out of bed, her mind racing as she thought of the children. Samuel had already beaten her to the door.

Show Illustration #3

Throwing it open, they saw thick smoke and flames licking at the roof. "There's no time to gather anything!" Samuel cried urgently. "We must get out now!" Susanna rushed into the hall, calling for their maid, Betty, to gather the children from the nursery. Being eight months pregnant, Susanna knew she would be of little help to the maid and that it was urgent for her to get out of the smoke. Rushing downstairs, Susanna tried to make it out the front door, but the wind was so strong that it blew the flames directly toward her. The heat was so intense! Three times Susanna tried to break through the flames but was driven back. Finally, on the fourth attempt, she gathered her skirts tightly around herself and forged ahead. She could feel the heat scorching her legs and face, but she pushed on. Suddenly she felt the heat subsiding and the cool night air hitting her face. She'd made it!

Susanna gazed wildly about, searching for Samuel and the children. No one! The yard was empty! She hurried around the side of the house, frantically scanning the garden. Relief flooded her heart as she saw several of her children standing a safe distance from the house. "Where's your father?" she asked as she gathered some of her littlest children in her arms. Patty, the second youngest, pointed to the house just as Samuel emerged, coughing and sputtering. "It's no use," he said, gasping for air. "John is still in the nursery. I could hear him crying but there is no way for me to get to him." Susanna felt like her heart was tearing in two as she thought about her little John left in the fire.

▶ **Show Illustration #4**

By this time several men from the town had gathered to help. Suddenly they heard a voice calling from the upstairs window. Looking up they could see John's little face peering out at them. Somehow he had managed to crawl up and break out the window! One of the men shouted, "Quickly! Let's see if we can make it up to him from the outside." There was no time to fetch a ladder, so one man was hoisted up on the shoulders of another. He pulled John into his arms just as there was a loud splintering sound. Suddenly the roof crashed into the nursery! The place where John had been only seconds before was engulfed in flames!

Susanna sank to the ground as she gathered John into her arms. "Thank you, God!" she cried aloud, as tears streamed down her face. "You've saved him, just like a brand plucked from the fire." She didn't know for what purpose God had allowed John's life to be spared, but in her heart she made a vow to particularly care for his little soul. *Lord, help me to teach him true religion and the way that he should live so that his life can bring You honor. And Lord, please give me the grace I'm going to need to do it carefully and sincerely.* Moments later, the whole Wesley family huddled together, watching their home go up in flames.

In the weeks that followed, work began on a new house. During that time, Susanna gave birth to their last child, a girl named Kezia. For the time being, the other children were sent to live with family and friends. Susanna dearly missed having her children with her.

Within a year they were able to move into a new home. While it was a much larger and solidly built brick house (see map), the cost of building it had only pushed them further into debt. Still, Susanna was just happy to have the whole family back together again. However there was much work to be done. She noticed that while the children had been apart, they had forgotten many of the habits she had worked so hard to establish.

In the past, eating had always been restricted to meal times, friends had always been monitored, her children had always been required to sit still during family worship. Bedtime had always been at 8:00 p.m. sharp. Now the children were used to looser schedules, more freedom and had become silly and rude.

For Susanna, these habits were more than just keeping an orderly home. They were ways to teach the children that life was not about serving themselves and being self-focused. She prayed that submission to these house rules would help lead them to submission to God's authority.

In order to help them with their behavior, Susanna decided to set aside time to individually meet with each child for one hour a week. She wanted to provide opportunities to have spiritual discussions with them without all the other children hearing their private conversation. In the process, she found that she got to know them better as individuals, which was something she treasured. As she began school lessons with her children and they grew accustomed to being at home again, Susanna's heart rejoiced to see them thriving once more.

● **Show Illustration #5**

"Charles! Pay attention!" Susanna's strong voice broke through the quiet afternoon, causing the other children in the classroom to raise their heads from their work. Charles shook his head to clear his mind from daydreaming and forced himself to pay attention to the work at hand. He knew it would do him little good to complain that he was tired of studying or that it was much too warm in the classroom to think. His mother would hear none of it. She worked hard to teach all of her children, and playing during school hours was most certainly not tolerated. Even from the time of his earliest memories, his mother had never given them anything they cried for. She gave them only what she thought was good for them. Even then they were required to ask politely for it. Charles snuck a quick peek out the window to see where the sun was in the sky and estimated it to be about 4:00 in the afternoon. *Only one hour left and then he'd be free! He could do this!* Diligently, he bent his head over his books.

Susanna smiled quietly to herself as she watched her children at work. *Oh, how she loved them!* Because of her firmness, she knew they didn't always understand that love. She felt her responsibility as a mother weighing heavily on her. At times she feared she would fail to be as committed as she ought. However, her children knew what to expect from her, and in turn, she made great efforts to praise and reward their good behavior. She was also a firm believer in keeping all promises that she made to her children and this helped them to trust her. Susanna checked the time: 5:00 p.m. on the dot. "All right children, you may put your things away. Let's sing a psalm and read from Isaiah 53. Then we'll be done for today."

As her children's sweet voices filled the room, Susanna saw how earnestly Charles sang. While they were too poor to have any instruments of their own, he had always loved music. She wondered how God was going to use that gift of his in the future.

▶ Many years passed.

One by one Susanna watched her children grow up and leave the home. Following a serious fall from a carriage, Samuel passed away, leaving Susanna penniless and in debt. This forced Susanna out of her home and left her to trust God

with her needs. Over the next seven years she went to live with her children, going from one home to the next.

Show Illustration #6

She continued to keep in touch

with her children by writing letters that offered advice, spiritual thoughts and love. Even though she gave advice, the older she grew and the more she studied God's Word, Susanna realized how little she actually knew! However, this did not stop her desire to pour her life into her children and to see them follow the ways of God. She knew that this alone would bring them happiness.

Her children wrote back, and by this method they kept in touch. However, while letters kept her informed, Susanna missed seeing their faces. She especially longed to see Charles and John. Both of them had become preachers and were busy traveling, so visits were few and far between. After one such visit with Charles at his home in Bristol (see map), she realized that every time she was around him, she was spiritually encouraged. So while his visits were seldom, she found she could never blame him. She knew that what he was doing was worthwhile and that God was blessing his ministry in ways she could never have imagined. And so it was that even while she missed her boys, she didn't wish for anything to change.

Show Illustration #7

Finally a time came when John was able to take a turn supporting his mother. He'd first established a church in Bristol (see map) but then moved to London where he bought a former cannon factory called *The Foundry*. He used a large part of it for a meetinghouse where he could hold services. The smaller part he turned into his living quarters. While there, Susanna began attending his services. Since the time that she had been a little girl she had only ever attended the Church of England where the emphasis was strongly on works. As she spent more time with John, Susanna became aware of the change that had come over both Charles and John. They now had confidence and assurance of their salvation which seemed to energize them. They trusted that salvation was a "gift of God, not of works" and that it was for "whosoever believeth."

One Sunday, as she sat in the meetinghouse listening to a guest speaker, Susanna heard the phrase "The blood of our Lord Jesus Christ which was given for thee." Suddenly she felt her heart struck by the profound truth that "God for Christ's sake hath forgiven you." Her salvation didn't depend on how good a person she had been. It was the work of Christ on the cross that saved her from eternal separation from God. It was His work and nothing more. She had to confess that sometimes she had acted like her salvation was dependent on her success or failure as a mother.

Bowing her head silently, she let the tears stream down her face. *Oh Lord, I have known You all these years, and yet I have never been hit so deeply by the fact that my salvation has nothing to do with my works. I have tried so hard to live a life that is pleasing to You and to teach my children to do the same. Yet that isn't enough. You are so holy and so perfect that nothing I could ever do would gain me the right to know You. Thank you that in Your perfect plan You sent me a Rescuer, Your Son Jesus Christ Who lived a perfect life in my place. I am accepted because of Him. Oh thank You!*

When Susanna was old and knew that her time on earth was coming to an end, she had one simple request: "Children, as soon as I am released, sing a psalm of praise to God." And that's just what they did. As soon as her spirit left this world, her children gathered around her bed. As they had so often done during their childhood school days, they sang a psalm together, praising and worshipping God.

Show Illustration #8

Many years later, John found himself kneeling in front of his mother's grave (see map), wishing he could talk to his mother just one more time. He wished he could tell her all that had happened to him and how much she had impacted the man he'd become. After John had realized that salvation was not by works, many other people also began to understand this truth. John didn't even realize what was happening when God began to use his incredible organizational skills. *The Foundry* was soon replaced by an even larger chapel in London (see map), but before he knew it he had become the leader of a worldwide movement known as Methodism. As a result, many people were growing in their understanding of truth.

John didn't know yet that he would preach over 40,000 sermons in his lifetime. He also didn't know that his brother, Charles Wesley, would go on to write 6,000 hymns, many of which we still sing today: "Depth of Mercy," "Jesus, Lover of my Soul" and the most popular one, "Hark! The Herald Angels Sing."

What John did know for sure was that he had been greatly affected by his mother's example.

As he read the words on her tombstone written by his brother, John nodded his head in silent agreement:

> "In sure and steadfast hope to rise,
> And claim her mansion in the skies,
> A Christian here her flesh laid down,
> The cross exchanging for a crown."

Susanna had endured many trials in her life and had very few possessions at her death, but now? Now, she was enjoying a heavenly home that could never be taken away.

In the little space of her home and her life Susanna had filled her children's lives with a godly influence. It was seen in her dependence upon God in those hard times. It was seen in the time, structure and advice she gave her children. It was seen in her own tender heart as God continued to teach her and help her grow in her own faith. As John stood there, he remembered what his mother had often said: "I am content to fill a little space if God be glorified."

John laid his hand on the stone and whispered, "To God be the glory."

Review Questions

1. In the beginning of the story, what was Susanna Wesley most worried about as she waited for her new baby to be born? *(Her family was very poor, and they had borrowed a lot of money.)*
2. How many children did Susanna and her husband Samuel have? *(She was pregnant with her 19th child, but nine of them had already died.)*
3. What bad news did Susanna's daughter Hetty tell her about her husband Samuel? *(He had been arrested and put in jail because he could not pay back the money he had borrowed.)*
4. Whenever Susanna put her apron over her head, hesr children knew not to interrupt her. What was she doing? *(Praying; she spent hours talking to God.)*
5. What terrible thing caused Susanna and Samuel to wake up in the middle of the night? *(Their house was on fire.)*
6. How was Susanna's son John rescued from the upstairs nursery? *(A man was hoisted up to the window and John was pulled out.)*
7. What did Susanna do after they were all together again in their new home to make sure she had time with each one of her children? *(She talked with them alone for one hour every week.)*
8. Who was the teacher for the Wesley children, and where did they go to school? *(Their mother, Susanna, taught them at home.)*
9. What was something that Susanna and her children did at the end of their school day that her son Charles especially loved? *(They sang a song of praise to God.)*
10. When Susanna's children grew up, her husband died and she was very poor. Where did she live? *(With her children, traveling from house to house)*
11. How did Susanna stay close to her grown children when she was away from them? *(She wrote them letters.)*
12. What special job did Susanna's sons John and Charles have? *(They were preachers.)*
13. When Susanna went to John's church, she heard something that made her realize that trying to be a good person was not the way for her sins to be forgiven. What was the way that she was saved? *(Trusting in what Jesus had done for her when He died on the cross)*
14. What did Susanna ask her children to do after she died? *(Sing a song of praise to God, just as they had done together when they were young)*
15. Discussion Question: Susanna Wesley depended on God through many troubles, and God used her example to help her sons Charles and John become men who told many people about Jesus. Do you think that doing a job that nobody sees is still important? Tell about someone who has made a difference in your life who may not have received a lot of praise for what he/she did. How do you think God might use the "small" choices you make to one day make a big difference? *(Encourage your class to share.)*

Map Notes

All of the images on the map are mentioned in the text, and are all related historical sites that still exist today.

- The Old Rectory–This is the house built for the Wesley family following the fire in the story. It was much larger and solidly built than the house destroyed in the fire. However, the expenses incurred in building it put the Wesley family farther in debt.
- The New Room Chapel–This is the oldest Methodist building in the world. John Wesley established a meeting house in Bristol in 1739, but the church soon outgrew it. The New Room Chapel was built in 1748 and is still used for regular service. It houses a museum as well.
- Charles Wesley's Home–Close to the New Room Chapel is the No. 4 Charles Street house, the home that Charles and Sally Wesley lived in with their family. It also houses a museum focused on the family and the history of hymn writing.
- John Wesley's Chapel–As mentioned in the story, the Wesley's first church in London was established at The Foundry, a former brass cannon casting site. In 1778 this new chapel was built nearby.
- Susanna Wesley's Grave–This is located in Bunhill Fields near the Wesley Chapel in London. Bunhill Fields is also the grave site of John Bunyan and Isaac Watts. The headstone pictured in the story was later replaced by a new headstone with a different inscription.

And whatsoever ye do in word or deed, do all in the name of the Lord Jesus, giving thanks to God and the Father by Him.
Colossians 3:17

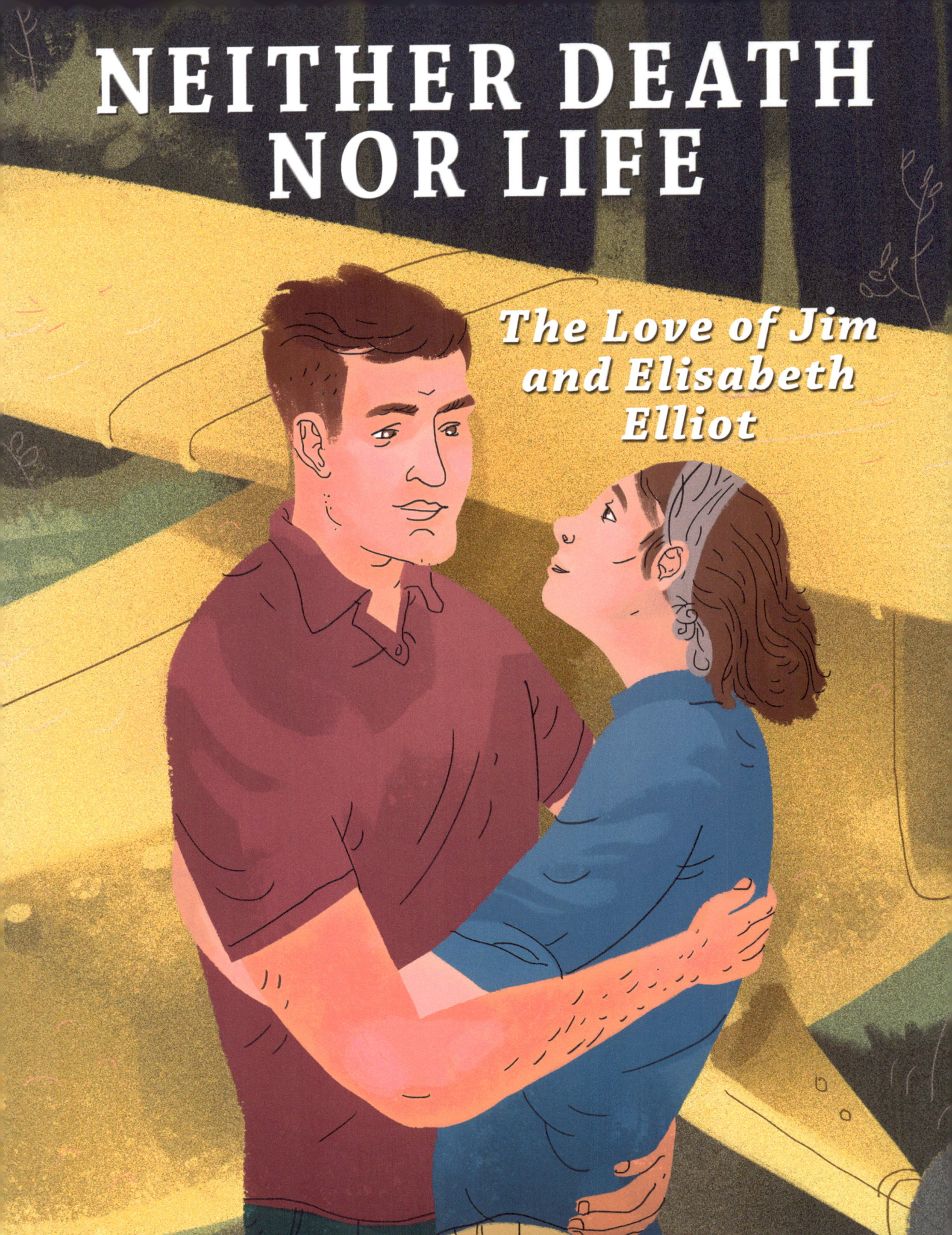

Inset (detail map)

- Shandia
- Palm Beach
- Curary River
- "Terminal City"
- Shell
- Meara
- Puyupungu

Main map

CANADA

UNITED STATES
- Portland, Oregon
- Chicago, Illinois
- Wheaton College
- Moorestown, New Jersey

MEXICO

Gulf of Mexico

North Pacific Ocean

ECUADOR ★ Quito

COLUMBIA

VENEZUELA

BRAZIL

PERU

NOTE TO THE TEACHER

This story may be told in two, five or six sessions.

The circle (●) indicates where to divide the narrative when teaching two sessions.

The triangle (▶) indicates the breaks for five sessions.

The star (★) divides the narrative into six sessions.

PRONUNCIATION GUIDE

Antasio	An-*ta*-zi-o
Auca	*Aw*-ka
Puyupunga	Poo-yoo-*pun*-ga
Quichua	*Ki*-chwa
Quito	*Ki*-to
Shandia	*Shan*-di-ya
Waodani	Wah-o-*dah*-nI

Show Illustration #15

The early morning sun in Portland, Oregon, beat down on the head of the young man who was pedaling as fast as his legs would go. The school bell began to ring, and without a second to lose Jim Elliot rounded the last corner, sliding on the gravel as he made the turn. In a big cloud of dust, he skidded to a stop and hopped off his bike. Offering a brief apology to his classmate, Fred, who was waiting to lock the bikes, he hurried inside the school building.

Jim Elliot wasn't ALWAYS running late. He was just running late MOST of the time. He was well known for his energy and speed, along with usually being a tad bit late. Jim smoothed back his brown, windblown hair as he rushed into his class. He was a good-looking young man with rugged features and a solid build, but this didn't really seem to make much difference to him. He slid into his desk, pulling out his books as he did so.

Normally he enjoyed school, but today he had a hard time concentrating as he thought about the conversation he knew was coming with John about the school dance.

The lunch bell rang and Jim, Wayne and Fred settled down with their lunches. Jim bowed his head to thank God for his meal. When he glanced up he saw Wayne and Fred looking at him strangely. He knew they didn't understand why he prayed. They didn't have a relationship with God, so they couldn't know.

Jim remembered the night his relationship with God had started. He had been six years old when he realized he was a sinner and that he needed Christ. He realized that day that Christ had died on the cross for his sins, and rose again, making it possible for him to have a relationship with God. Afterward he had declared to his mama that the Lord Jesus could come whenever He wanted because he was ready now.

Jim smiled at the memory and shifted in his seat. He wanted Fred to have a relationship with this Jesus he had come to know. Jesus meant everything to Jim.

Show Illustration #16

"Hey Wayne, you coming to the school dance?" Jim looked up from his sandwich to see John, the president of the student body, approaching their table. *Oh no*, he thought preparing himself for the pressure he knew he also was about to receive from this popular six-foot athlete. Wayne ducked his head and muttered something about having too much going on right now. John sighed. "So Jim, what about you? You're in this student body as much as I am and ought to support it."

There were some bad things that would be going on at the school dance, like smoking and drinking. Jim knew it was no place for a Christian to be. He knew what he needed to say. "Yes, I'm in the student body but not the way you are. I'm a Christian and the Bible says that I'm in the world but not of it. That's why I'm not going to the dance." Nobody said anything, and for a moment, it was so quiet you could have heard a pin drop. The student body president studied him for a moment, then backed off and apologized for mentioning it.

The older Jim got the more he realized how much he needed God. So many of his friends were looking for satisfaction in other things: money, careers, sex, friends, etc. Didn't they know a relationship with God was fulfilling?

When Jim graduated from high school he decided to attend Wheaton College in Illinois. (Show map.) Even though Jim would be at a Christian school, he knew he still needed to make a deeper commitment to the Lord. He didn't want to just know a lot about God or spend time with Him only at church. No, he wanted to be entirely committed to God every day, no matter what the cost. Little did he know how much would be required of him in order to keep that decision.

★ Show Illustration #17

It started in little things, like choosing carefully what foods to eat. Jim ate fruits and vegetables and fewer desserts. Then it spread to making time for exercise by setting his alarm each night so that he'd have time to spend with God in the morning. The commitment to God also affected the way Jim interacted with girls.

"Jim, how come you don't go out with girls on the weekends, like the rest of us?" his friends would ask him.

"This is the time in my life when I can get to know God better," Jim would reply. "And besides, I trust God enough to know that if He thinks I need a girlfriend, He will bring one along for me without my having to play the bloodhound."

However, what was most curious to Jim was that despite his decision to stay away from women, he found himself enjoying conversations after class with a certain Elisabeth Howard (or 'Betty' as her family called her). She was an intelligent woman, and he liked her honesty. She wasn't afraid to disagree with him if she saw the need to do so. When Elisabeth's brother Dave invited Jim to spend Christmas at their house in Moorestown, New Jersey, he readily agreed. (Show map.)

▶ Show Illustration #18

Jim enjoyed the time with their family and enjoyed getting

– 31 –

to know Elisabeth better. They often stayed up late after the rest of the family was in bed, discussing their views on issues like war, women, church, poetry and missions. He had been realizing recently that God had given him the command to "Go and preach the gospel." Through some of the things he'd been learning in his different classes he felt as if God was leading him to the foreign mission field–he just wasn't sure where.

Christmas break ended and they went back to school where the rest of the semester flew by. Jim was interested in Betty, this much he knew. Yet he also knew that God had to be first and he wanted nothing to come between him and his Saviour, even someone like her.

One cool evening, months later, the two of them strolled down a quiet street, discussing what God had been doing in their lives.

"Doesn't it seem strange that we've been on only one date?" Elisabeth commented.

"Has it only been one?" Jim asked.

"Yes, remember? We went to the missionary meeting in Chicago last month together, but that has been the only official date we've been on."

"I guess you're right! We've spent so much time studying and talking together that we have become best friends: I hardly even realized it was happening."

Suddenly, as Jim was speaking he knew the truth. He loved Betty. He looked at her now, her sweet face smiling up at him, and he saw it in her eyes. She loved him too.

Jim looked up and stopped walking. Without realizing it they'd entered an old cemetery. Jim and Betty sat down together.

Show Illustration #19

"Betty, I've committed you to the Lord, just as Abraham trusted God with his son Isaac when God asked him to do a very hard thing. I care deeply about you but don't know what God has in store for you and me. I want Him to lead."

Jim could see Betty's eyes widening. "Jim, that's the exact same illustration I've been thinking of recently when I've been thinking about our relationship!"

Jim and Betty agreed that God was directing and if He chose to lead them together or apart, they would hold the relationship with an open hand, willing to let go if necessary. However, this was easier said than done.

★ When Jim and Betty decided not to write to each other over break, they found that surrendering each other was not a one-time thing. This tested their love for God and for each other. When they went back to school in the fall, they realized they were still good friends and if anything, their love for each other had grown. However, that love would be tested again.

At the end of the next school year, Betty told Jim she was headed to Canada for the summer. Jim's heart sank.

"I think it will be a great experience for you, but I'm going to miss you," he admitted, then added, "Would you mind if we wrote each other a little more this summer?"

Betty smiled. "If you think it's a good idea, I'd love to."

Jim responded frankly.,"To be honest, it scares me to know how quickly you can take God's place in my heart. I need to follow God to the mission field, even if He calls me without you."

"I understand, Jim, and I agree," Betty said softly. "So let's be careful to guard our hearts and go forward carefully."

While Betty was in Canada, Jim met a jungle missionary who told him that it was really impossible for him to have a wife in his kind of mission work. Jim took this as a sign that he should not marry Betty yet, since he was going to be doing rough jungle work too. Looking back, Jim was glad he had waited instead of rushing ahead of God's timing.

To fill his free time Jim read the stories of men and women who had served God. Over and over he saw that people who were truly in love with Christ did not find it hard to give up things in this life. He felt challenged even in his love for Betty. How he struggled to not want his own way. Suddenly he was struck with a certain thought, so profound yet so simple that he sat down with his journal and wrote it out quickly before he would forget it. "He is no fool who gives what he cannot keep, to gain that which he cannot lose." *Why yes!* He thought to himself. *That's just it! Anything I may give up here on earth is only being given up in exchange for something better! Something I can never lose! My relationship with Christ! Oh how sweet is the love of Christ!*

The very next day Jim was reading a letter from a friend telling him that he was leaving the mission field in Ecuador because of his wife's health. Jim knew they would need someone to fill this position. He responded by writing and offering himself for the work. As Jim scanned his letter, he decided it had been written too quickly. He didn't want to act without God's leading, so he decided to wait until he'd prayed about it more and God had given clearer direction. In the meantime, Jim wrote Betty telling her all about it. He knew she would be praying for him too.

While waiting to make a decision, God led Jim to a linguistics school where he could learn valuable skills about different languages. It was there that he met a missionary from Ecuador who told him about an opportunity.

Show Illustration #20

"Jim, have you heard about the Aucas? They are a savage group of Indians. These people have been untouched by other civilizations and have driven back every white man who has ever tried to reach them! They go naked, use bark cloth to carry their babies, sleep in hammocks and steal machetes and axes when they kill our Indians. They are dangerous, but Jim, they need the Lord!"

▶ These words weighed heavily on Jim's heart. Was God leading him to Ecuador? Jim decided to pray for ten days asking God for direction. At the end of the ten days he knew the answer: "Go."

Jim wondered what all of this would mean for Betty and him. He knew God had been directing her heart toward the South Seas, which was not at all in the same direction as Jim. But he still loved her, more than ever. Why would God call them to two different places?

★ However, between visits to Betty a very strange thing happened. The doors were shut for Betty to go to the South Seas! Some people thought they should get married and go to Ecuador together. But Jim and Betty still felt the answer was no for now. However, Jim encouraged her to pray about coming to Ecuador on her own, despite what people might think of them. For four weeks Betty prayed and then the answer came for her too: "Go."

As Jim was preparing to leave for Ecuador, he specifically prayed that God would confirm his call by providing the fare for his trip. One afternoon as he left the post office he ripped open some letters to find multiple checks inside! He couldn't believe how much had come in! He still needed a little bit more for the trip but God was certainly providing! The next day a friend asked him to pick up some purchases. Jim gladly did and afterward he was given a $50 check.

Show Illustration #21

Jim headed home and put the money with the checks he had received from the day before when suddenly it hit him. Between all of the checks there was a total of $315 which was the exact cost of his trip! God had provided for his needs all within 24 hours, from five separate sources! Jim was greatly encouraged by how God was working!

Before long both Jim and Betty arrived in Ecuador. (Show map.) They lived in Ecuadorian homes across the street from each other. Jim got to see Betty almost every day as they studied Spanish, went mountain climbing, sightseeing, etc. Once again, Jim thought about getting engaged. However, the words of the missionary that it is a great impossibility to have a wife, kept coming to his mind. He wrote in his journal: "Marriage is not for me now. It simply isn't the time. I don't say and never did say it's not the thing for me. With tribes unreached which I now believe reachable only by unattached men, I will not do this thing."

One of the problems of reaching the Aucas was that no one knew where they lived. Imagine Jim's excitement when he was invited to go on a survey trip to the very area where people suspected they might live. As the plane took off, Jim's adrenaline kicked in. Eagerly he looked out the window as the plane lifted from the ground. Before long the plane was dropping to get a closer look among some trees, then moving quickly upward again, pulling out. His stomach dropped, but it was such a thrill! After several trips with no success, Jim was praying for a miracle. Without God's help, the Aucas would never be reached. In the meantime, until God opened that door, Jim continued to work with the Quichua Indians who were more easily reached.

After five months of living near Betty, Jim really wanted to marry her. He struggled with his emotions though, because he didn't feel it was God's will yet. A few weeks later he found out why.

●▶ Show Illustration #22

God led Jim to Shandia, a mission station in the jungle (see map). While in Shandia, Jim realized it would indeed have been hard to have a wife with him. He was so busy helping to build an airstrip and working with the natives that he would have had no time for her. Also, the natives had no sense of privacy and would often walk right into his house with no warning! Jim found himself being constantly interrupted by people coming to the missionaries for medical help: a boy with a broken wrist, a man with a machete cut, a breech baby case, etc. He didn't mind too much though, because he was continuing to learn the language as he interacted with these Indians he called brothers.

Although he was glad he was not married yet, Jim saw that eventually things in Shandia would be established enough that Betty would be able to join him. He decided to propose.

★ A month later Betty was sitting at home when the sound of hoofbeats broke through the night. She opened the door and saw a friend standing there. "Telegram for you, Betty. It's from Jim," he said with a knowing smile. She eagerly opened it and was surprised by the simple message. Jim was waiting for her in Quito. What could that mean? Betty had her suspicions and headed there as quickly as possible. A few days later her suspicions were confirmed when Jim got down on his knee in front of a fireplace and asked Betty to marry him. She said yes.

Even though God had led them to engagement, He continued to test their faith. After having an X-ray Betty was told that she had a very active case of tuberculosis. This was very serious and Betty thought for sure this would call off all marriage plans. Even if she would recover from this sickness, a life in the jungle would not be recommended for her. However, Jim's plans had not changed. "God has not led us this far to frustrate or turn us back, and He knows how to handle tuberculosis," he wrote in his journal. Jim had to head back to the jungle, but a week later he heard that their faith was rewarded! Further testing showed the tuberculosis had disappeared from her lungs!

Now all they were seeking was God's timing for their marriage, and He showed it in a very unique way. That June was an extremely rainy season in Shandia. For five days and nights in a row it rained and several large mud slides happened close by. Jim and the other men in their area began preparing in case the water started to rise. One of the men ran up to Jim breathlessly.

"Jim, the new house we built thirty feet away from the cliff is now only 15 feet away! The mud slides are just eating away at the forest and trail. If this rain keeps up, we'll have to leave and find a safer place."

Jim's stomach sank as he thought of all the work that they'd poured into the school buildings, the clinic and the kitchen. He didn't want to leave it all behind. He prayed for the rains to stop.

Show Illustration #23

However, the rain kept up for more than a week and it became evident they had no other choice but to go. They decided to try to save as much as they could. Jim was just ripping the screens out of the kitchen window when a lightning bolt streaked across the sky. With a loud crack the front porch disappeared into the river! Jim decided it was time to get out and scrambled to safety as quickly as he could. Behind him, the waters washed away the buildings and part of the landing strip. Shandia was gone.

Betty came to help in whatever way she could by sorting, collecting and drying things. The missionaries wondered if God was redirecting them through the loss of Shandia. They decided to try to find a spot to set up a new station. Betty stayed behind to guard the equipment. When they returned, Jim met Betty with excitement.

"Betty, we met an Indian man named Antasio who begged us to come and live with them and to build a school! This is the first time the Indians have asked us for help!"

"Oh Jim, that's wonderful!" Betty exclaimed. "Who is going to start that station?"

"That's the best part!" Jim said with a grin. "Ed and his wife are just starting to learn the language so they don't feel they can take on a new work. Another one of the unmarried men will be needed to help with the language and running the station here. So who do you think they picked?"

Betty smiled, knowing the answer. "So, how soon will you go?"

Jim's grin widened. "Well . . . how soon will you marry me?"

Jim and Betty together would be perfect for this mission. It was time for them to get married. God had worked it out in His timing and in His way. Three weeks later, after a simple ceremony, they became husband and wife.

Show Illustration #24

After their honeymoon, they began to prepare for the move to Puyupunga (see map). When they arrived, they were greeted by Antasio, who was grinning from ear to ear. The people were extremely welcoming, giving them food and shelter right away. However, the shelter had cockroaches, and Jim and Betty couldn't stand up in it because they were too tall. Betty was glad they were being so kind, but she wasn't really interested in sharing her home with cockroaches. So Jim set up a 16-foot tent that would be their home for the next five months. They had lots of work to do. With building a house and an airstrip, along with running a school for ten children, Jim and Betty were busy, but they continued to pray that God would bring people to Himself.

When summer came Jim and Betty closed up the little school and said good bye to their new friends. They were headed back to Shandia to help rebuild a more permanent headquarters for the missionaries there. While there, they received news: some Auca homes had been spotted!

▶★ Excited by the sighting, the missionaries began discussing ideas about how to let the Aucas know they were friends. They knew that these savages were dangerous and had already killed a number of people.

"Is it possible to lower gifts from a plane?" someone suggested. "Then maybe after a while they would look forward to our visits enough that we could visit them in person, bringing more gifts along?"

Show Illustration #25

Everyone liked the idea, so they decided to try it. Time after time, they dropped gifts, things such as articles of clothing, machetes, pots, beads, etc. "Oh God," Jim prayed, "Help these people to come to know You. Help them to have the relationship with You that I so enjoy. Lord, many Quichuas have heard, but the Aucas have never heard. Help us to know how to reach them. Amen."

One day, to Jim's delight, the Aucas sent some gifts back! The missionaries felt it was time to meet them face-to-face. Nate Saint, the pilot, felt confident that they could land safely on a beach that had been discovered. The men would go without the women for this first trip, because of the danger.

The night before flying out, Jim and Betty discussed the trip.

"Jim, what if you never come back?" she asked.

"If God wants it that way darling, I'm ready to die for the salvation of the Aucas," Jim told her.

Show Illustration #26

The next morning came all too quickly and everything was ready. Jim slung his bag up across his shoulder and headed for the door. Betty almost said, "Do you realize you may never open that door again?" but kept her mouth shut. This was not the time for that. Jim closed the door behind them and they headed down the trail. As Jim walked confidently and determinedly in front of her, Betty realized again how much she loved him.

They arrived at the landing strip. In a matter of minutes Jim was kissing her good bye, boarding the plane and taking off. Betty breathed a quick prayer: "God, may Your will be done. Jim knows the cost that is involved with this. Whatever happens, help the Aucas to see You."

Two days later Jim and his friends arrived in Palm Beach (see map) and were on the lookout for the Auca Indians. Jim wondered what it would be like to finally meet one in person. It was midmorning and already so hot that Jim felt as if he was sweating just from turning the crank on the radio. He decided to take a break and write a quick note to Betty. He wanted to tell her that their hopes were up but they had seen no signs of their neighbors yet. Little did he know that this would be the last letter he would ever write to her.

On January 6, Jim finally met the Aucas face-to-face. He smiled at the three naked savages who stood staring at him and his four friends. He was trying to be as friendly as possible. As Jim held out his hand and shook the hand of an Auca, he could not help but feel like shouting for joy. At last! At last! The Aucas and Americans were meeting! How he wanted to share the gospel with these Auca people, to call them his brothers in Christ. He knew beyond a shadow of a doubt that God had a plan for these people.

And he was right.

Yet Jim would not get to see all that God was going to do. Two days later, the men that Jim had prayed so hard for killed him and the four others. Jim gave his life for the Aucas, yet he would not have considered it a sacrifice. He had known the sweetness of Christ's love for him, and following God had been a privilege.

A few days after hearing the news of Jim's death, Betty finally received the letter that he had written to her at Palm Beach. Tears coursed down her cheeks as she read his words:

"Perhaps, today may be the day that the Aucas are reached," Jim had written, his excitement bubbling over. Through her tears, Betty couldn't help but smile when she saw that he had signed the letter, "Your lover, Jim."

Her heart ached. "Oh Jim," she whispered to nobody. "How I am going to miss you." And yet, strangely enough, amid all the pain, she felt a sense of peace. All along throughout their relationship Jim and Betty were committed to keeping God first. And now, even though Jim was gone, God was not. He remained her Comfort and Friend.

"God, You are enough," she prayed. "You called Jim and me to the Aucas, and I'm still willing to go if that is what You want me to do."

Show Illustration #27

And years later she did just that. Betty and her little daughter Valerie returned to the Auca people, and many of the Indians came to know the Christ that Jim had been so in love with. Their many prayers had been answered! And so, while Betty had lost a husband, the Aucas had gained a relationship with Jesus Christ. Jim was right:

"He is no fool who gives what he cannot keep to gain that which he cannot lose."

Epilogue

Elisabeth continued to serve among the Auca (Waodani) and Quichua Indians of Ecuador for several years before returning to the United States in the mid-1960s. There she encouraged and challenged believers through public speaking, writing books and a radio ministry. Her radio broadcast always began with her saying, " 'You are loved with an everlasting love'–that's what the Bible says–'and underneath are the everlasting arms.' This is your friend, Elisabeth Elliot."

Elisabeth remarried in 1969 to Addison Leitch, a professor at Gordon-Conwell Theological Seminary. He died in 1973 and Elisabeth married again in 1977 to Lars Gren, a hospital chaplain. They served and traveled together for many years until Elisabeth began to suffer from dementia and poor health.

On June 15, 2015, at the age of 88, Elisabeth died. Like Jim, she is ever in the presence of the Lord she loved and who has forever loved her.

Review Questions

1. What was one of the commitments Jim made in order to follow God? *(Eating mostly fruits and vegetables and few starches and desserts; making time to exercise; getting up early in order to spend time with God; refusing to chase after girls)*
2. Which did Jim and Elisabeth establish first, a friendship or a dating relationship? *(Friendship)*
3. What did Jim and Elisabeth discover when they decided NOT to write each over the summer? *(That surrender is not a one-time thing; that their love for each other actually had grown)*
4. Why did Jim and Elisabeth decide to proceed cautiously in their relationship? *(They realized how quickly their feelings could overcome their faith. They wanted God to remain first.)*
5. What did Jim do to fill some of his free time? *(He read stories of men and women who served Christ.)*
6. What phrase did Jim write down when he was struggling with surrendering Betty? *("He is no fool who gives what he cannot keep, to gain what he cannot lose.")*
7. While Jim was at linguistics school, whom did he meet? *(A missionary to Ecuador)*
8. When Jim wasn't sure of where God wanted him to be a missionary, what did he do? *(Prayed for ten days)*
9. How did God confirm Jim's call to go to Ecuador? *(God provided the exact amount of money that Jim needed for his fare, from five separate sources and all within 24 hours.)*
10. Why did Jim continue to wait when it came to the decision of marrying Elisabeth? *(There were tribes that could be reached only by an unmarried man.)*
11. What kind of demands did Jim have while working in Shandia that would have made it very hard for him to have a wife? *(Built an airstrip; worked with natives; helped the natives with medical needs, etc.)*
12. Once Jim had proposed, what made Betty think the marriage plans were going to have to be called off? *(She became very sick with tuberculosis.)*
13. What made Jim and Betty realize it was the perfect time for them to get married? *(A husband and wife were needed for the mission of living among the Indians and starting a school. No one else was available.)*
14. What did the missionaries do in hopes of befriending the Auca Indians? *(Dropped gifts from a plane)*
15. The night before the dangerous expedition, what did Jim tell Betty when they discussed the possibility of his being killed? *("I am ready to die for the salvation of the Aucas.")*
16. After Jim was killed, what did Betty do? *(She returned to live and work among the Auca Indians.)*
17. Why would Jim not have considered his death a waste? *(Because many Aucas came to know the Christ he loved)*

For I am persuaded, that neither death, nor life, nor angels, nor principalities, nor powers, nor things present, nor things to come, Nor height, nor depth, nor any other creature, shall be able to separate us from the love of God, which is in Christ Jesus our Lord.

Romans 8:38, 39

OUR FATHER'S HOUSE

A Story of John Paton

Show Illustration #35

"Tell us about the time you were almost eaten by cannibals, grandfather!"

"Or the time you had to hide up in a tree all night!"

"Or what about the time the man pretended to be sick and then tried to attack you with a knife!"

John Paton looked into the eager faces of his two grandchildren. He certainly did have plenty of stories he could share with them about his time as a missionary to the islands of Vanuatu, but there was another story he wanted to share. Through all that had happened over the many years, there was one face he remembered most, one voice it seemed as if he could still hear.

"Tonight, children," he began, "I want to start by telling you about someone whose story deserves to be told much more than mine–my father's.

Show Illustration #36

"I was born into my father's house in 1824 as the oldest of five sons and six daughters. Our home was in a place called Torthorwald, Scotland. The house was made of heavy oak wood, stones and a roof of wood and strong grasses woven tightly together. It was not a fancy place because my father, James Paton, didn't have much money. Inside the house, there was one big room where my mother worked. That room was our dining room, kitchen, living room and bedroom all in one! The other room was my father's workshop, and ours as well. We all worked together on big wooden machines to weave socks to sell to the storekeepers.

Show Illustration #37

"Between these two rooms was one other tiny space that we called 'the closet.' This was a special place where my father would go to pray. After each meal was over he would go into that closet and shut the door. All of us children always tiptoed by so we wouldn't disturb him. Sometimes we could hear the sound of his voice as he talked to God."

"What did he talk about?" asked one of the children.

"Oh many, many things, but what I remember especially is that he prayed for me and my brothers and sisters. He prayed that we would know God and love Him. Of course, I knew my father loved God because he talked to Him so much. That's why he always had a smile on his face."

Do you know God? I pray that you know that He loves you and that He has made a way for you to be His child. The Bible says in 1 John 3:1: "Behold, what manner of love the Father hath bestowed upon us, that we should be called the sons of God." That's great news that should bring a smile to your face.

The children had seen that same smile on their grandfather's face, too.

John continued, "But my father didn't always pray by himself. Every morning and every evening he would gather our whole family together and we all would pray and read God's Word, the Bible. There wasn't anything that could make him forget to do this. One thing I especially remember is that he would get down on his knees and ask God to help all the people in faraway parts of the world who had never heard about Jesus to have a way to learn about Him."

"Like the people in the islands where you went as a missionary?" asked the girl.

"Yes, and sometimes my father would cry when he prayed. God used those prayers in my heart to make me want to go and tell those people about Jesus.

Show Illustration #38

"On Sundays we would walk four miles with father to church. It was a long way and too hard for my mother to walk, but we didn't mind the distance at all. Afterward we would hurry home to mother to tell her everything we had learned about God. Then my father would tell all of us an exciting story from the Bible or about Christians who had lived many years before. Those Sundays were very happy, special days."

"Our family worked hard from early in the morning till late at night to make enough money to live. By the time I was 12, I had started to help my father with his work. I also had made two important decisions. The first was to trust the Lord Jesus as my Saviour from sin."

Listening to John talk, you might think: "Wasn't He good enough already? He had a good father who prayed all the time, and he went to church and read the Bible–wasn't that enough for John to be right

---

GOSPEL POINTS

God's unconditional love

Jesus is the only perfect Son of God.

All have sinned.

Jesus' sacrificial death on the cross

Jesus has risen again!

Will you repent and accept Jesus as Saviour?

Application for the believer

Throughout the text of this story, we have included Gospel Point icons. Beside the icon(s), there will be suggestions to help you explain that gospel point to your class. These points are optional with the understanding that you may plan on presenting the gospel during your Bible lesson time instead.

However, if this story is the only lesson being presented, please take advantage of this feature. Sow the gospel seed!

with God?" No, John knew it wasn't. He knew that despite those things, he had disobeyed God in his heart and often chosen to do wrong things. He had sinned: and the truth is that you and I have sinned too. Romans 3:10 says "There is none righteous, no, not one." We all say, think and do things that do not please God. Sin is very serious to God because He is holy–perfect and without sin. He promises to punish sin which means we face separation from God forever when our life on earth is over. We need Jesus. John had learned that He needed Jesus as well, and that's why he had believed on Him to save him from his sins.

"The other important decision I made was to be a missionary. I would go to a land where people had not heard of Jesus so I could tell them the truth about God."

"That was when you met the cannibals, wasn't it grandfather," whispered his granddaughter with a very serious look on her face.

"Not quite yet, my dear," he said, patting her head. "First I had to go to school. . . ."

"I remember very well the day when I had to leave my family and go to the big city of Glasgow, where I would have a job teaching the poor people in the city about God and going to school at the same time.

"I had to walk for many miles before reaching the train that would take me to Glasgow. My father walked with me for the first six miles. At first we talked about loving and obeying God, but then my father became very quiet."

"Was he tired, grandfather?" asked the boy.

"No, I could see that his mouth was moving and I knew he was silently praying for me. There were tears running down his cheeks, too."

Show Illustration #39

"When we finally got to the place where we had to part, my father took my hand and said, 'God bless you, my son! May my God help you and keep you from all evil!'

"After one last hug good-bye, I turned and ran down the road, too sad to say anything. Just before I came to a bend in the road, I turned and looked back. There was my father still standing where I had left him, holding his hat in his hand as he always did. I waved good-bye and rounded the corner out of sight. Then I sat down by the side of the road and cried."

The grandchildren gathered around John. They could see even now there were tears on his face.

"After a short while," he said, "I arose and climbed a hill nearby to see if my father was still there, and at that very moment I saw him climbing a hill to look for me! He didn't see me: after a few moments he climbed down and disappeared from my sight. I made a promise that day, children. I promised that with God's help I would always live in a way pleasing to the father and mother God had given me. I've never forgotten that promise.

"After working as a missionary in Glasgow for ten years, I heard a pastor talking about how much the people who lived in the New Hebrides islands (now Vanuatu) needed someone to tell them about Jesus. Many of these people had never heard of what Jesus had done for them and were living in fear and in the darkness of sin."

 Maybe you don't know who Jesus is either. I want you to know that He is the sinless Son of God. That doesn't mean that He's another God. Jesus Himself said in John 10:30, "I and my Father are one." He is without sin and He is God! John wanted the people of New Hebrides to know Jesus.

"Right away I felt that God was telling me that I should be the one to go. But many people told me it was too dangerous–that I might be eaten by the cannibals!"

"That was old Mr. Dickson, wasn't it grandfather?" asked the little boy. "Tell us what you said to him!"

A little smile formed on John's face. "Well now . . . I told him he'd probably die one day soon and be eaten by the worms in the ground."

The children giggled.

"And I said that as long as I served the Lord, it didn't seem to matter to me if I was eaten by cannibals or by worms. We'll both have new bodies in Heaven just like Jesus our Saviour who rose from the dead!

"Even so, children, I still wasn't sure God wanted me to go, so I decided to travel back home and ask my parents what they thought. I'll never forget what they said. They told me that they had been praying ever since I was a baby that I would be a missionary. After hearing that, there was no doubt in my mind that this was what God wanted me to do.

"So in 1856, at age 33, I sailed with my new wife to the island of Tanna and began work as a missionary there.

▶ Show Illustration #40

"Children, I could never have imagined how hard the next five years would be. My wife and little baby boy soon died from a sickness they caught on the island. The Tannese people killed each other as they continued fights passed down from their fathers and their fathers' fathers. Many of them didn't want to hear about the true God, or believe that they should obey Him. Sometimes they threatened to kill me and the other missionaries."

The children grew very still as their grandfather continued.

"I watched as many of my dear friends were killed, died of illness, or became very sick from fear and worry. I, too, was often sick and thought that I would die. Many times I was alone, but even then I could still call upon our great Heavenly Father. And I did, again and again. I also continued to tell the people of Tanna the truth about God–how much He loved them and how He could be their Heavenly Father."

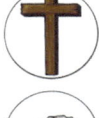 *What John told these people is true for you as well. God loved you so much that He sent His only Son, the Lord Jesus, to die on a cross made out of wood and to give His blood as payment for our sins. Isaiah 53:6 says ". . . and the Lord [God] hath laid on him the iniquity [sin] of us all." Because Jesus was sinless, He could take on Himself all the wrong things that you and I have done and be punished in our place. And just as He became sin for us on the cross, through your trusting in Him, you can have all His goodness applied to you. That means that in Christ you can be declared righteous before God. You can completely trust in Jesus because after He died and was buried in a tomb, three days later He came out of that grave alive again. He is alive today, and He will never die again. Jesus did all of this so that you could be forgiven of your sin if you believe in Him. He did this for the people of Tanna as well. That is what John continued to tell them.*

John continued with his story. "Finally, children, it became too dangerous for me and the few remaining missionaries to stay on the island of Tanna, so I had to leave. But I was not going to give up. One day I knew I would go back to the islands."

"While back in Scotland, I met a lady who also wanted to be a missionary in the New Hebrides, and soon we were married."

"That was grandmother, wasn't it," asked the little girl.

John smiled. "Yes dear. Before we left for the islands, we made one last visit to see my parents."

Show Illustration #41

"Together, we knelt down to pray with my mother and father in their little home in Scotland. My father asked God to care for us and to keep us safe. When he finished and we stood up to say good-bye, I knew it would be the last time I'd see them again in this world. I think they must have known that too. As your grandmother and I left that day, we asked God to make us the kind of people my parents were. It was four years later as I was working far away as a missionary, I heard that my father had died. He was 77 years old."

"That's how old you are now, isn't it grandfather?" asked one of the children.

"Why yes, so it is! Although your grandmother and I were still young when I went back to the New Hebrides for the second time. This time we went to the island of Aniwa. It was still a dangerous place, like Tanna, and there were many times I thought we'd be killed. I remember how the people watched us build our house and plant banana trees.

"There was one old chief, named Chief Namakei, who was especially interested in what we were doing. One day Chief Namakei told me that all the people had thought we would die because we'd built our house on ground that they thought was special to their gods. He said, 'Our fathers told us the gods would be angry and would kill anyone who built a house there. But we watched and you did not die! Our fathers told us anyone who ate bananas planted there would drop dead, but you planted bananas, ate them and did not die. What our fathers have told us is not true,' Chief Namakei continued. 'Our gods can't kill you. Your Jehovah God is stronger than the gods of Aniwa.'

Show Illustration #42

"Then something wonderful happened, children." John leaned forward in his chair. "Chief Namakei gathered his people and began to pray. He looked up to Heaven and said, 'Father, Father, our Father.' Now he did not understand all about the Lord Jesus yet, and he was still confused about many things. Remember children, he didn't have a father, as you and I do, who loved God and taught him how to pray. But he had learned that God could be his Father."

Maybe, like Chief Namakei, you don't have a father who loves God or who does what is right. Maybe you don't get to be with your father very much, or you don't even know who he is. But if you have repented of your sin and trusted in what Jesus did when He died on the cross for you, then you need to remember what Chief Namakei learned. God is your Father. God promises that when you have believed on Him, you become His child, a part of His family. He sent His son Jesus to this earth for that purpose. Galatians 4:4-5 says "God sent forth His Son, made of a woman, made under the law, To redeem them that were under the law, that we might receive the adoption of sons." God is a Father who will never disappoint you or leave you alone. He will always love you.

"Many years went by. As your grandmother and I continued to teach the people about God, things began to change on Aniwa. More and more people came to believe in Jesus as their Saviour. Families began to be different. When we first came to Aniwa, the people thought that there was nothing wrong with killing your baby if you did not want it. I knew of three people who had killed their own children–two because they were angry, one for no reason at all. But as each of these people came to believe in the Lord Jesus, they each decided to adopt little babies that had no parents to care for them and make them part of their families.

Show Illustration #43

"Soon crowds of people began to come to the church services we held for them. They listened carefully as I told of Jesus' life and death. Instead of praying to gods made out of stone who could not hear them, the people began to pray to their loving Father in Heaven. Families began to have a special time to pray every morning and every evening, just as they saw us do with our family, and just as my father had done with our family many years before. Children and grown-ups started going to school to learn how to read and write, something they had never heard of before. Whenever someone did something wrong, the chiefs would decide with their people what the fair punishment would be, instead of killing each other in angry fights. Now there was much less stealing and fighting.

"By the time your grandmother and I left the island many years later, every person on Aniwa had put his/her trust in the Lord Jesus as Saviour. You see, children, God had answered the many prayers of my father from that little house in Scotland."

Show Illustration #35

John gathered his grandchildren in close to him and placed his arms around them.

"Some days I miss my father's house and all the wonderful memories of that place. But it will not compare to another house I'm going to soon. There I'll see my father again, and Chief Namakei and all those from Aniwa who believed in Jesus . . . and you too if you've placed your faith in Him. Yes, children, we'll spend eternity praising the Lord in Our Father's house."

Will you be there with them one day when your life on earth is over? Have you ever believed in the Lord Jesus to save you? Do you know that you have done wrong things and that you deserve to be punished? Do you believe that Jesus died on the cross to take the punishment for your sin and that He came alive again? Are you ready to turn from your sin and to trust in Jesus to save you? The Bible says in Acts 16:31, "Believe on the Lord Jesus Christ, and thou shalt be saved." You can believe in the Lord Jesus today.

Maybe you know that you have already trusted Jesus as your Saviour, and you know He has forgiven you of all your sin. Then you should always remember that God is your Father. No matter what kind of father you have here on earth, God is the Father who will never disappoint you or leave you alone. Would you like to take a minute right now to thank God for being your loving Father?

REVIEW QUESTIONS

1. Where did John Paton grow up? *(Torthorwald, Scotland)*
2. What did John Paton's father and his family make in their cottage home? *(Socks)*
3. What was the "closet" used for in their home? *(A place for the father to pray)*
4. What two important decisions did John make by age 12? *(To trust Christ as his Saviour, to be a missionary)*
5. What things did John's father do to be a godly influence for his children? *(Prayed for them consistently, led the family in worship, took them to church)*
6. Where did John Paton go to be a missionary? *(Vanuatu or the New Hebrides Islands; Tanna and Aniwa also acceptable)*
7. Why did some people discourage John from going to Vanuatu? *(There were cannibals who lived there.)*
8. What sad thing happened to John soon after he arrived on Tanna? *(His wife and son died.)*
9. Why did John have to leave Tanna? *(It was too dangerous. The people did not believe in Christ and tried to attack him.)*
10. Why did Chief Namakei watch John carefully when he planted a banana tree? *(To see if John would die when he ate the fruit)*
11. What changes occurred on Aniwa as the people believed in Jesus and called on the Heavenly Father? *(Took care of unwanted babies, ended idol worship, became educated, family worship, settled disputes without fighting)*
12. What was the house John knew he was going to soon? *(Heaven)* Who would he see there? *(His father, Chief Namakei, all who trust in Jesus)*

That which we have seen and heard declare we unto you, that ye also may have fellowship with us: and truly our fellowship is with the Father, and with His Son Jesus Christ.

1 John 1:3

www.ingramcontent.com/pod-product-compliance
Lightning Source LLC
Chambersburg PA
CBHW041538220426
43663CB00002B/76